Jazz Figures
for Individual and Group Practice

by Denis DiBlasio

ISBN 0-7935-9948-2

EXCLUSIVELY DISTRIBUTED BY

HAL•LEONARD®
CORPORATION
7777 W. BLUEMOUND RD. P.O. BOX 13819 MILWAUKEE, WI 53213

Visit Hal Leonard Online at
www.halleonard.com

INTRODUCTION

Teaching improvisation in a jazz ensemble setting is just plain hard to do because its so time consuming. A large part of the learning is done alone, so when one student is soloing the other 20 kids are just sitting there counting the lights or throwing things. The book in front of you is designed to consolidate information that your entire group can use while at the same time making your practice time more productive. **This book will not only work for the individual but for any group of players in any combination.**

Exercises are not laid out in order of difficulty but in a smattering of basics that are part of the jazz language. Any exercise can follow any other. Exercises can be used as warmups, technique work outs, drills for improvisation or patterns that are memorized then applied to the chords at the beginning of each chapter.

Even numbered pages are on the left and odd on the right. The left side is treble clef while the right hand side is bass clef. All exercises are laid out chromatically or in the cycle of fourths. By laying it out this way any instrument can sit next to any other instrument and be able to use the same book. The student simply starts at the proper line for his or her instrument. Concert instruments start at the symbol **(C)**, Bflat instruments **(Bflat),** and Eflat players at **(Eflat).** Once at the bottom of page simply go to the top line and continue on. The pages marked **"Non group"** are for individual practice. These pages keep the format of the book in line while offering different types of useful melodic material.

SOME IDEAS

1. After drilling for a while go to the chord sheet at the beginning of the selected chapter and play the exercise while looking at the chord sheet only.

2. Have the rhythm section keep a groove going while the others play the exercises. Change tempos and styles. (All exercises are accompanied by the chord changes they apply to).

3. **"Real Life"**. This is great for testing. If a student makes even one mistake you have to go to the beginning and start again. (Sometimes one exercise last 50 minutes). ha ha

4. Players start on random lines to create different harmonies that will eventually render you insane.

5. Repeat each line a specific amount of times (ex. 4 times) before moving on to the next line. This enables the wind players to give their chops a break by missing a line when fatigued.

TABLE OF CONTENTS

Major scales in chromatic order (Non group)

1. Major (ascending).

Scale and ninth chord

Scale and ninth chord

Scale in thirds

Scale in thirds

Scale in fourths

Scale in fourths

Major -5 starting on the 13th

Major -5 starting on the 13th

4th pattern

4th pattern

Major 7-5 chords (Non group)

2. Major (descending).

Diatonic chords

Diatonic chords

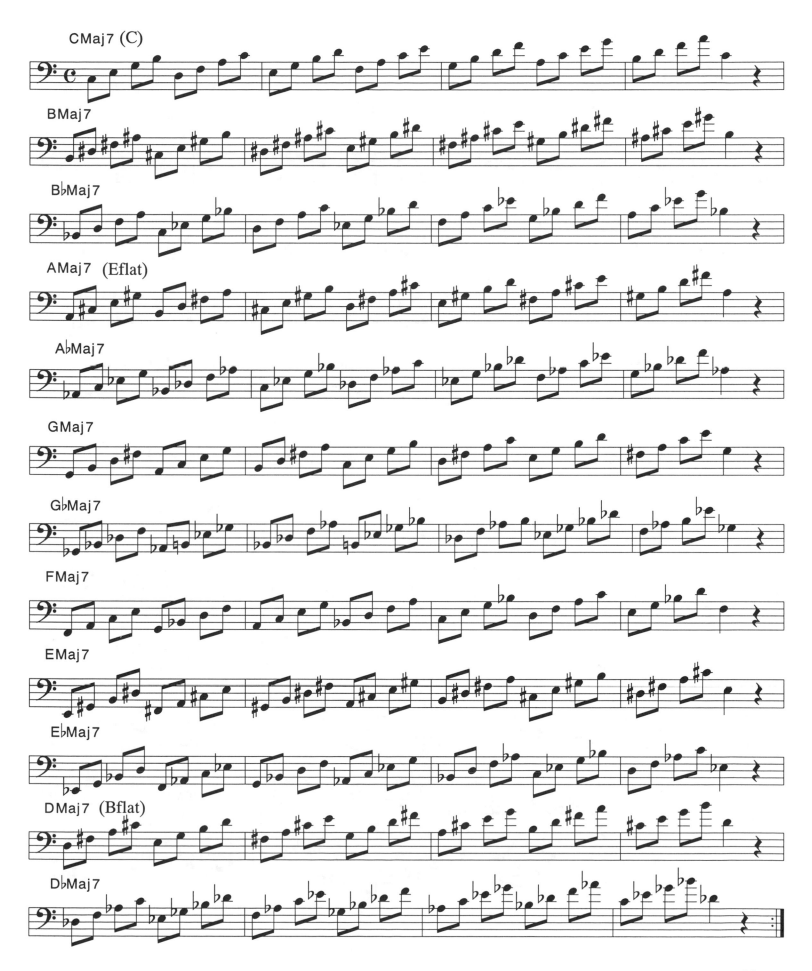

Diatonic chords/ascending and descending

Diatonic chords/ascending and descending

4th pattern (2)

4th pattern (2)

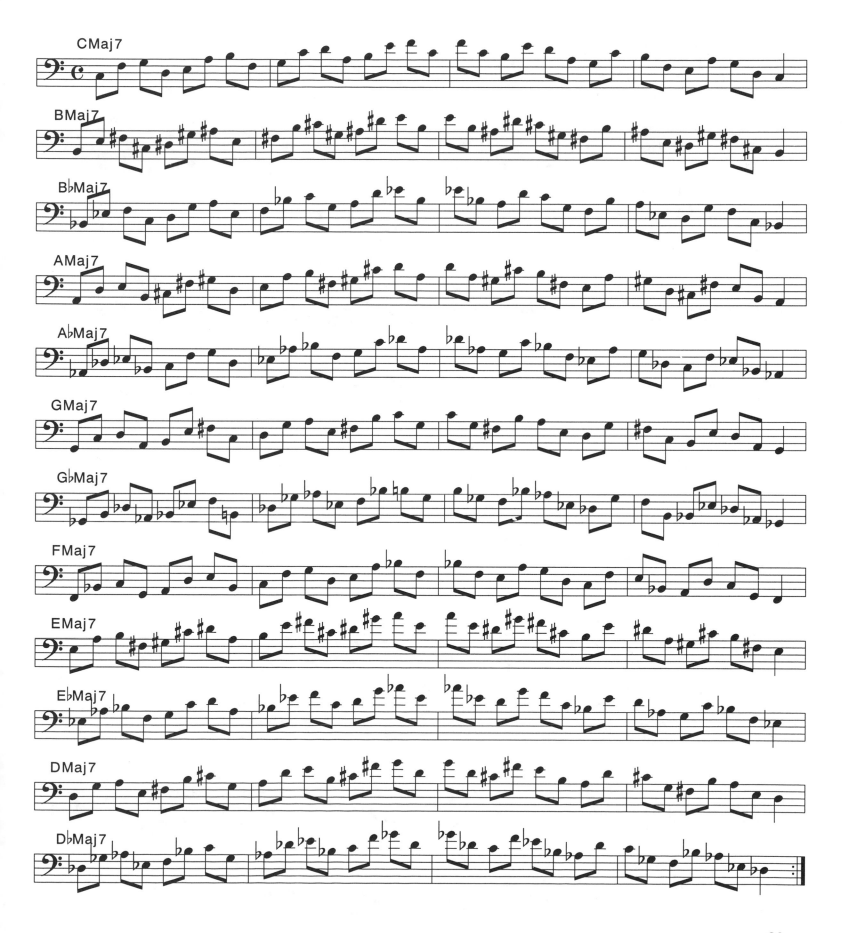

Major BeBop Scale a la Dave Baker

Major BeBop Scale a la Dave Baker

Major BeBop no.2 a la Dave Baker

Major BeBop no.2 a la Dave Baker

4ths in groups of 3 (Non group)

3. Major (one measure each).

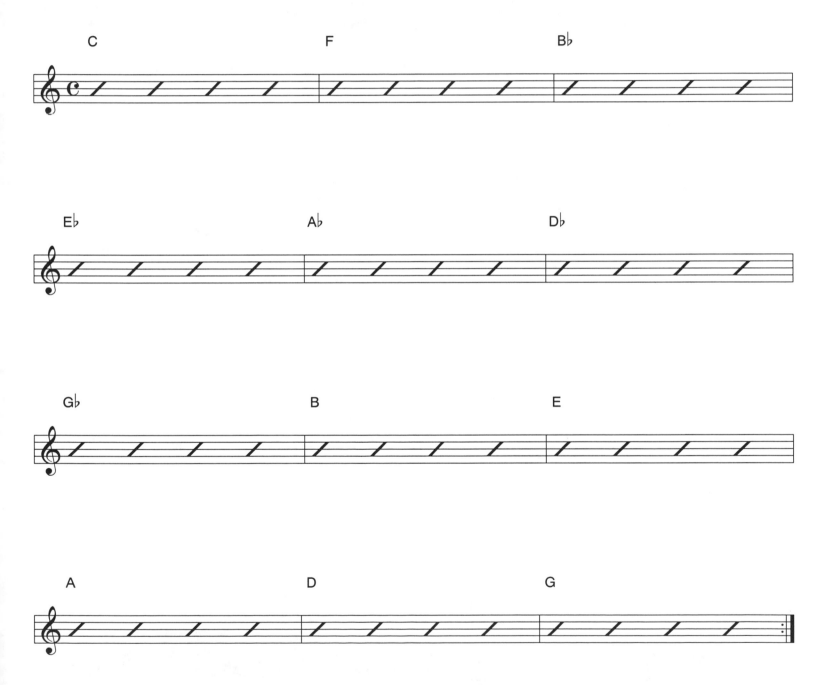

Double time in major

Double time in major

Major BeBop

Major BeBop

Major pentatonic

Major pentatonic

Major pentatonic (2)

Major pentatonic (2)

Chromatic Bebop line

Chromatic Bebop line

Major triads (Non group)

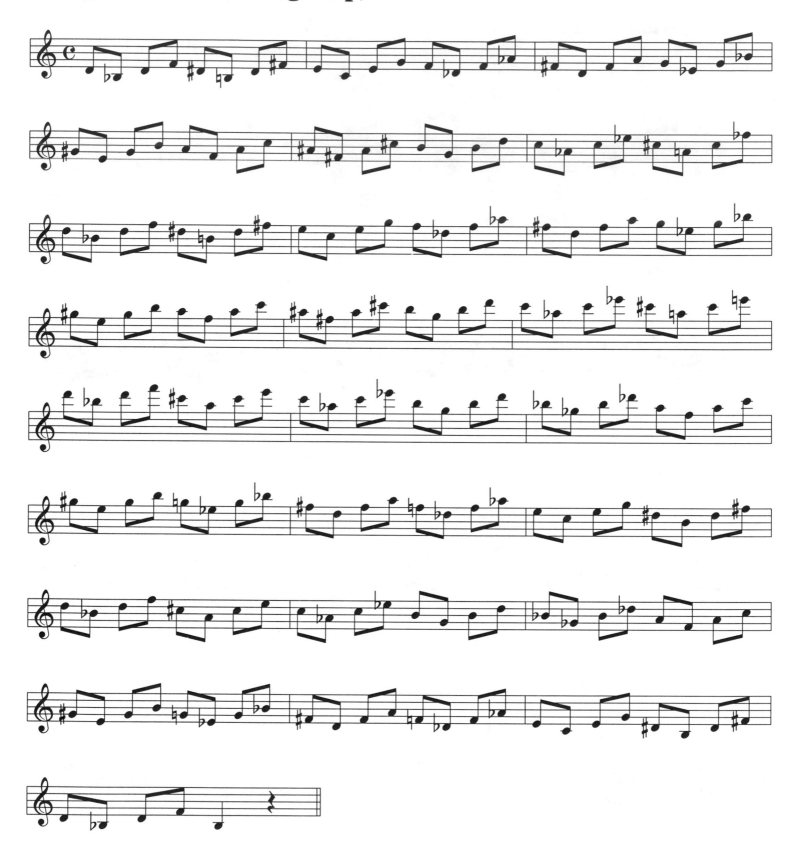

4. Major and Minor

13th chords

13th chords

Scale exercise

Scale exercise

Scale exercise 2

Scale exercise 2

Bebop scale

Bebop scale

Bebop exercise 2

Bebop exercise 2

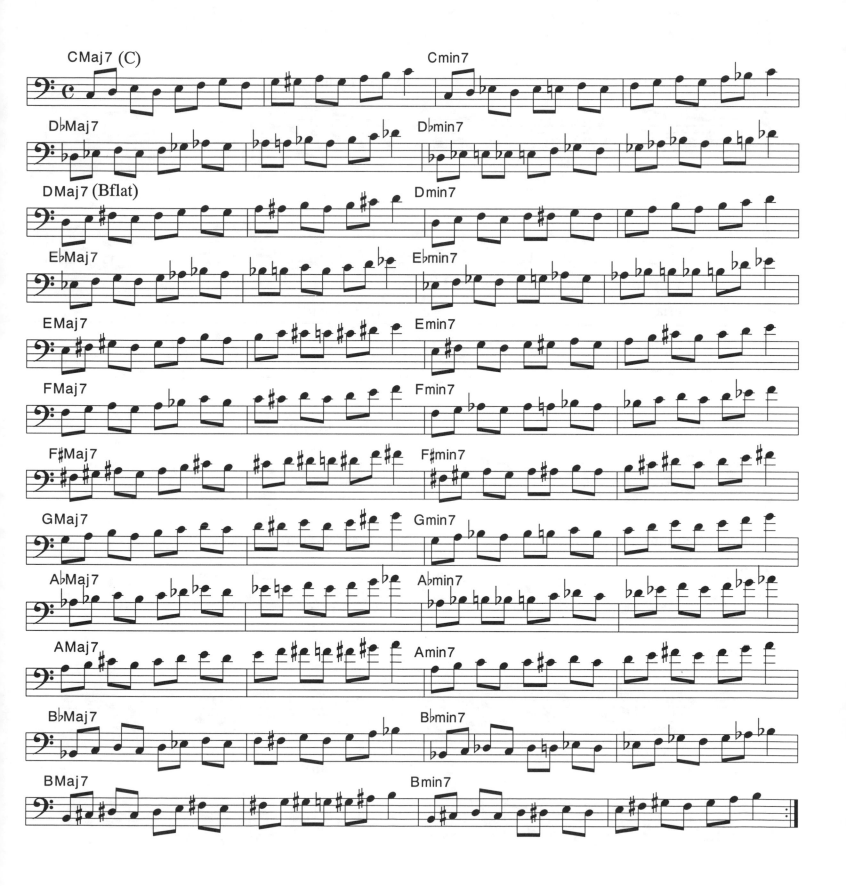

Running scales (do in all keys) (Non group)

5. Altered Dominants

Altered scale

Altered scale

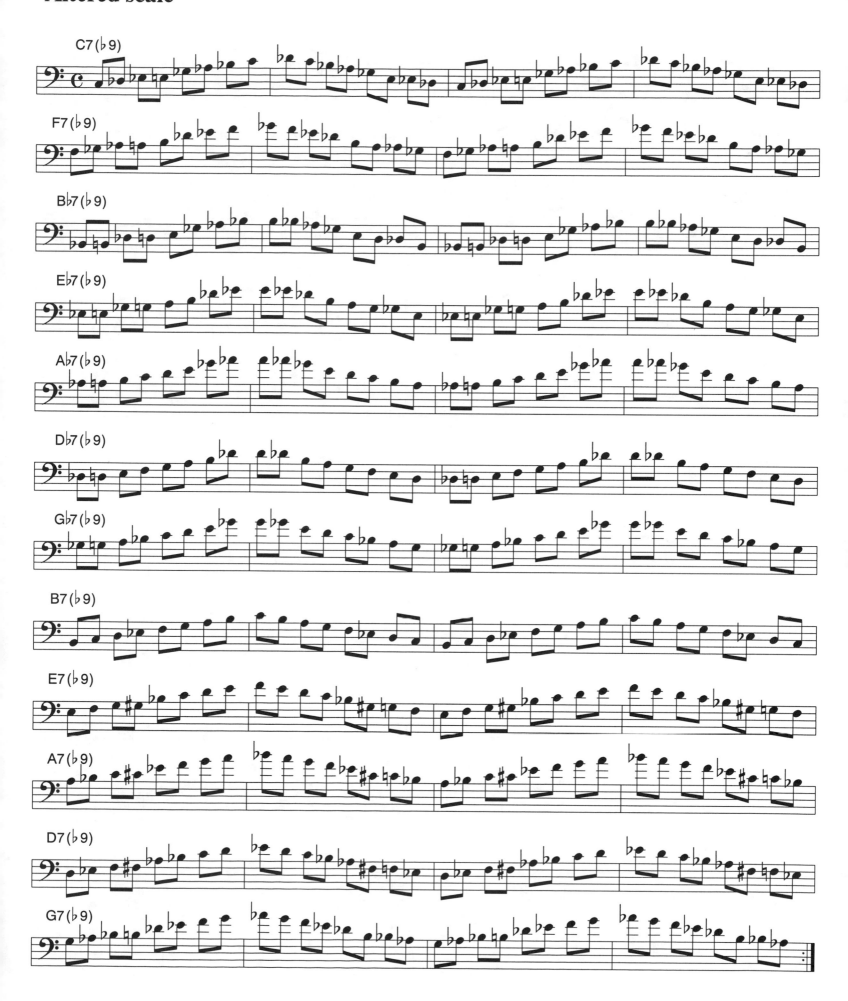

Alt. arpeggio 1,3,-5,-7,-9,+9,-13,+9,-9,-7,-5,3

Alt. arpeggio 1,3,-5,-7,-9,+9,-13,+9,-9,-7,-5,3

Altered scale in thirds

Altered scale in thirds

Altered scale exercise

Altered scale exercise

Altered scale exercise 2

Altered scale exercise 2

Chromatic 4ths (Non group)

6. Dominants (two measures each).

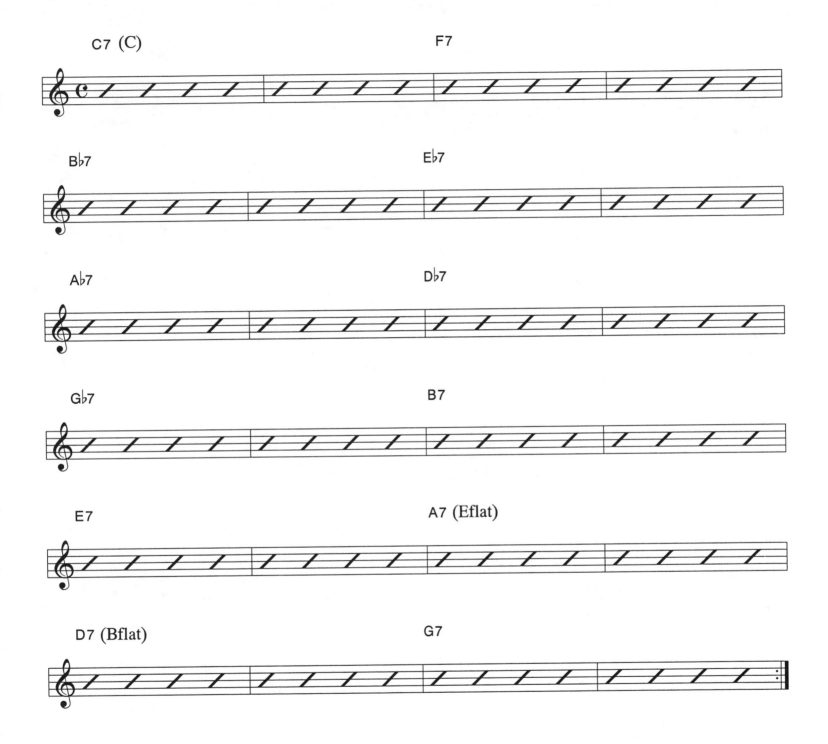

13th chord

13th chord

13th chord +11

13th chord +11

Dominant Bebop scale

Dominant Bebop scale

Bebop scale exercise

Bebop scale exercise

Scale in 4ths

Scale in 4ths

Chromatic workout (Non group)

7. Dominant (one measure each).

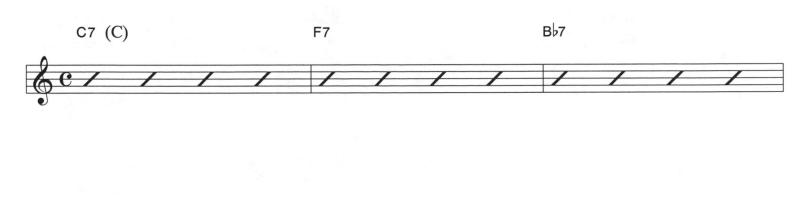

Bebop scale exercise

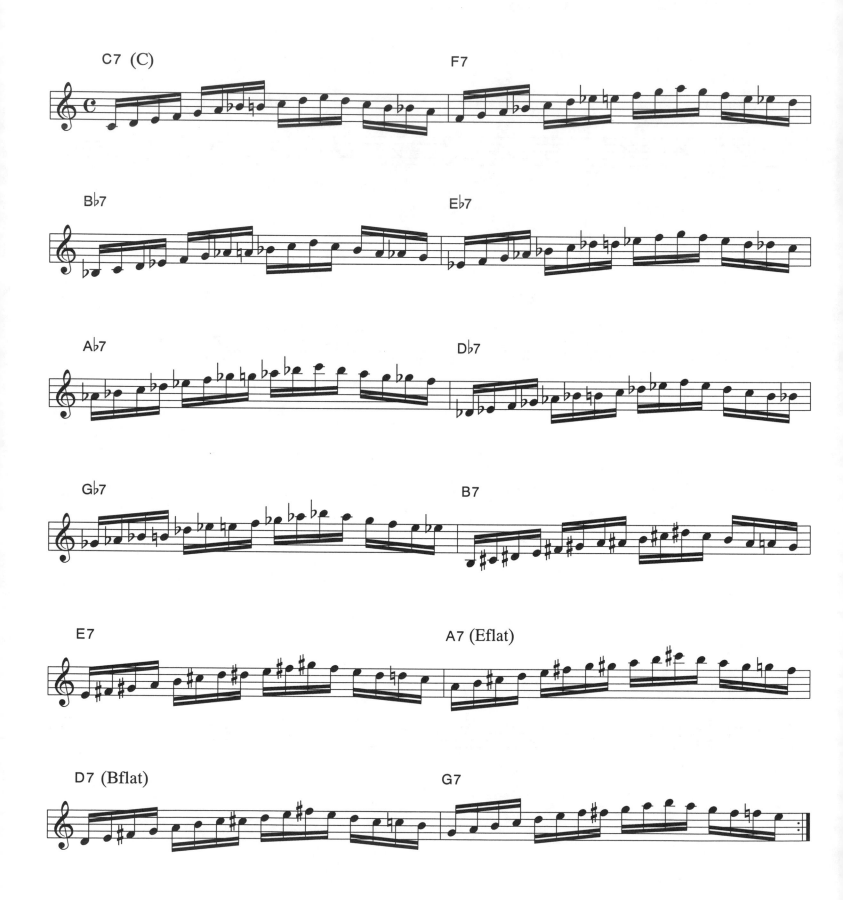

Bebop scale exercise

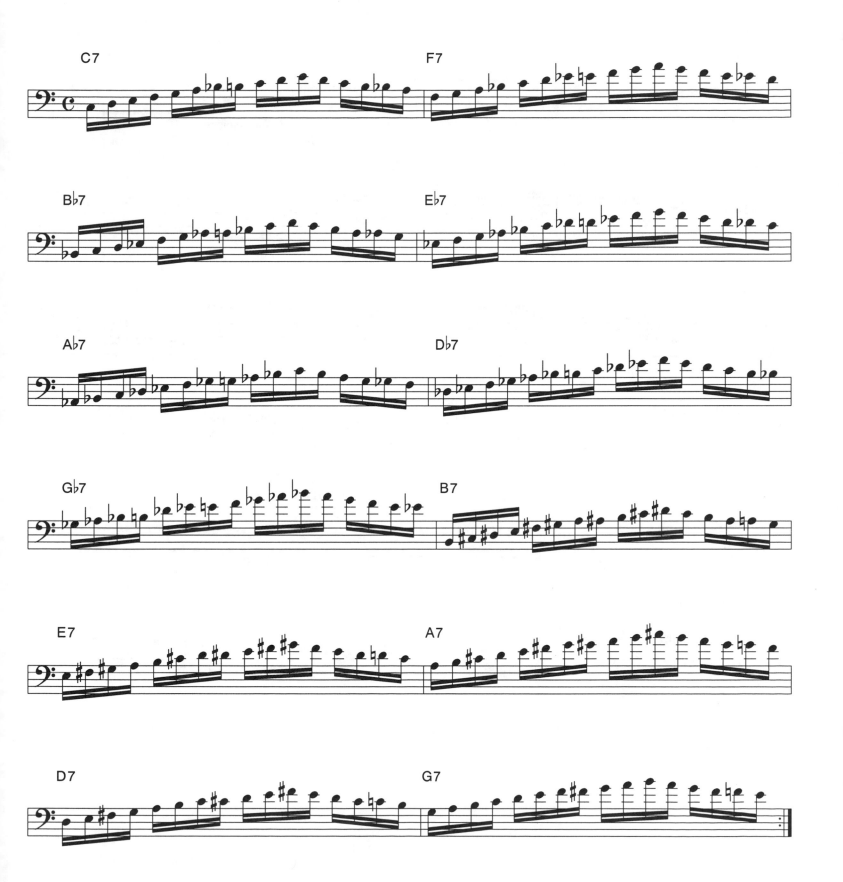

Bebop scale exercise 2

Bebop scale exercise 2

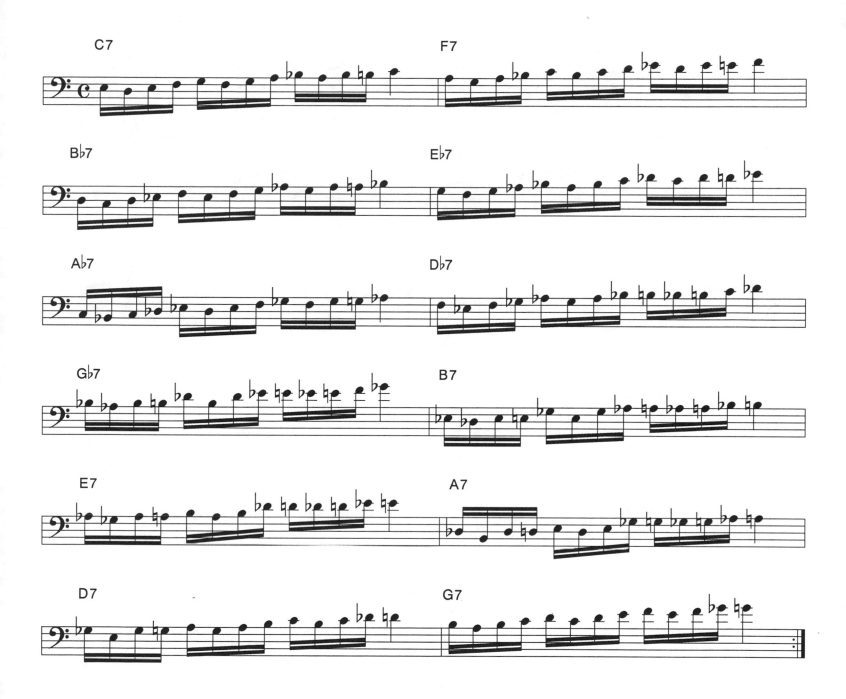

Bebop scale exercise 3

Bebop scale exercise 3

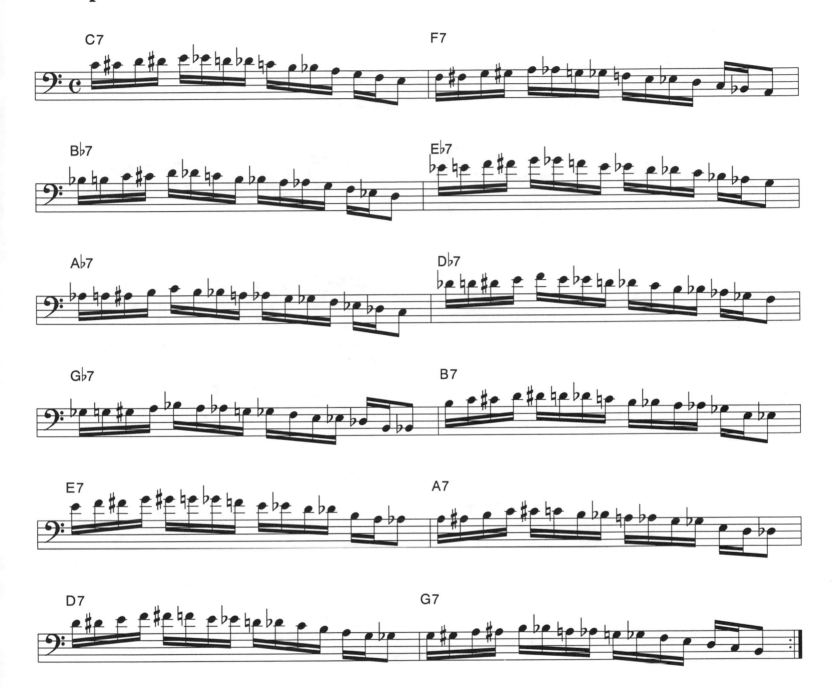

Chord to 9th then scale

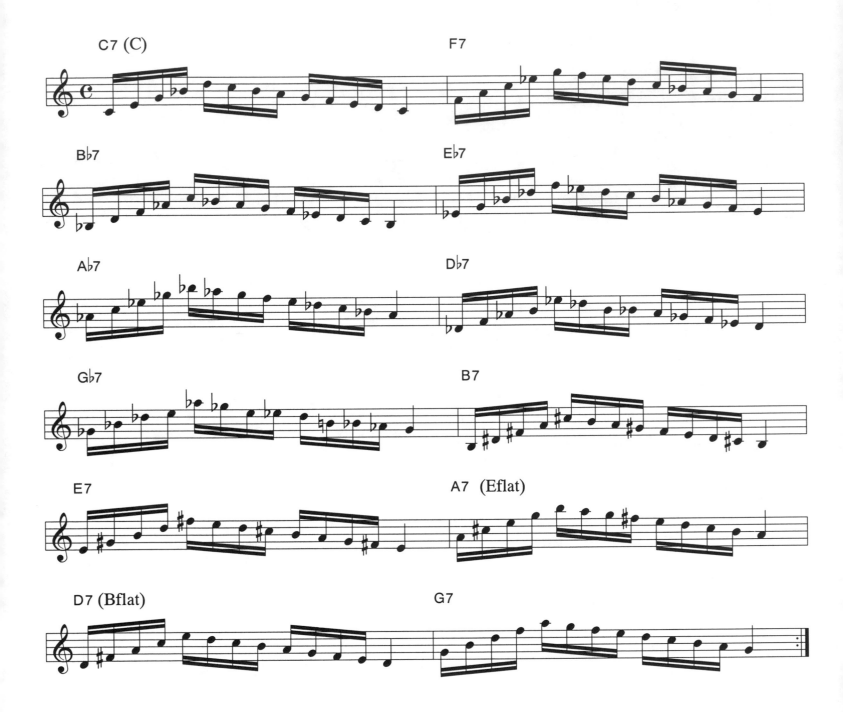

Chord to 9th then scale

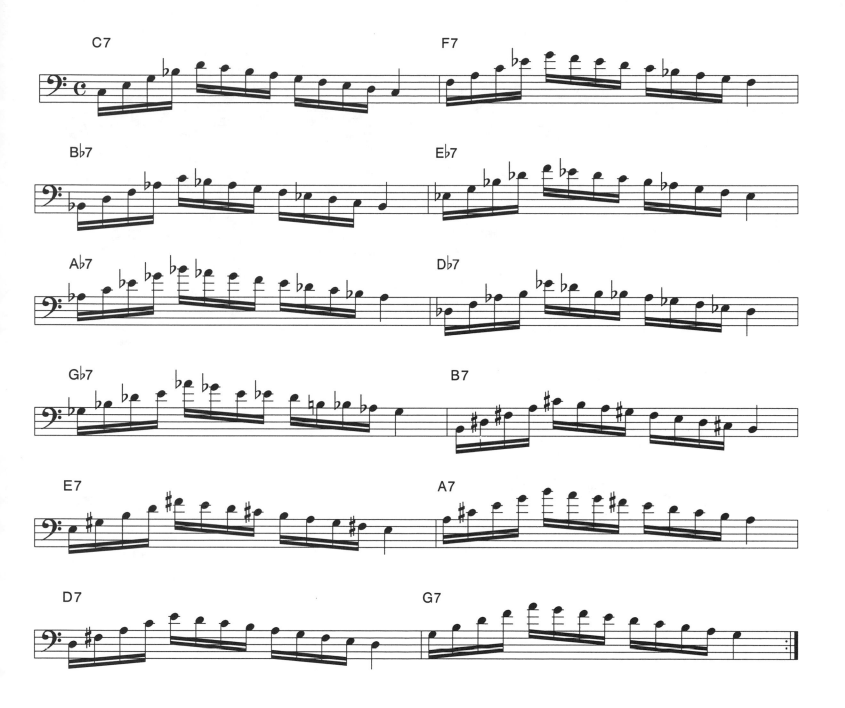

13th +11 chords descending

13th +11 chords descending

Chromatic exercise 2 (Non Group)

8. Minor

Cmin7 (C)

C♯min7

Dmin7 (Bflat)

E♭min7

Emin7

Fmin7

F♯min7

Gmin7

A♭min7

Amin7 (Eflat)

B♭min7

Bmin7

Scale to the 9th

Scale to the 9th

Scale in thirds

Scale in thirds

Scale exercise

Scale exercise

Triads

Triads

Bebop scale

Bebop scale

Chromatic exercise 3 (Non group)

9. Minor 7-5

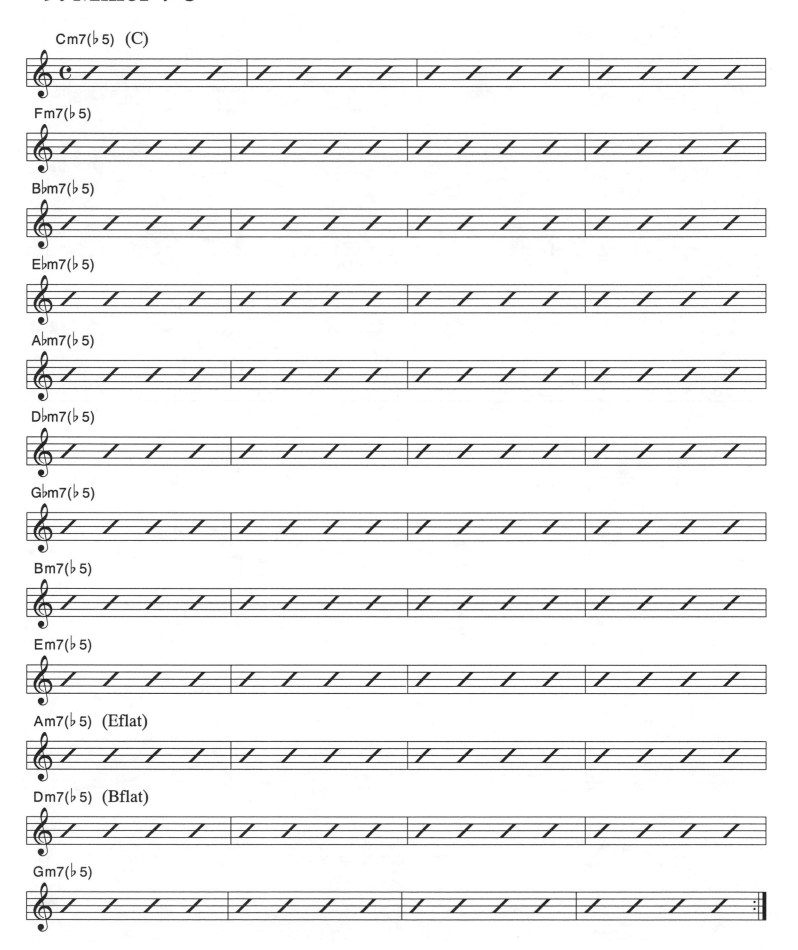

Locrian mode

Locrian mode

13th chord

13th chord

Chromatic line off the flat five

Chromatic line off the flat five

9th chord and scale

9th chord and scale

Scale exercise

Scale exercise

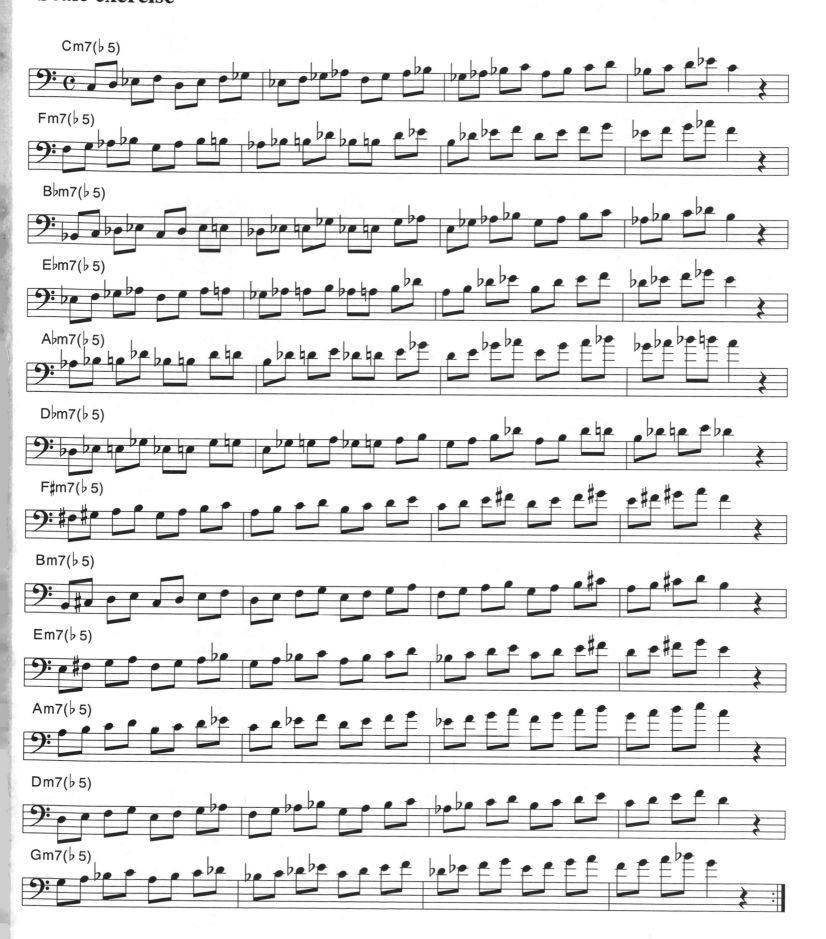

111

Major Blues Tunes in All Twelve Keys
by Jordon Ruwe
Contains 12 standard blues tunes with solos in all keys. Includes four-measure excerpts in all keys and jazz lines and exercises in all keys.
00030444 ....$12.95

Minor Blues Tunes in All Twelve Keys
by Jordon Ruwe
Twelve original tunes, scale systems for improvisation, four-measure riffs and exercises highlight this instructional volume.
00030437 ....$14.95

A Simple and Direct Guide to Jazz Improvisation
by Robert Rawlins
Helps musicians know what to do with specific chords in specific contexts. Lays out clear and objective guidelines on how to turn scales and chords into real music. Perfect for a college or high school improvisation class!
00841046 ....$14.95

Stylistic Etudes in the Jazz Idiom
compiled by Lou Fischer
120 etudes composed by 7 respected jazz performers/educators. Contains 5 etudes each in swing, ballad and Latin/funk categories, beginning at a medium level and progressing in difficulty. Includes a total of 15 etudes each for saxophones, trumpet, trombone, bass trombone, piano, guitar, bass and drums.
00841045 ....$28.00

Talking Jazz/Playing Jazz
TELLING A STORY THROUGH
YOUR JAZZ IMPROVISATION
by Peter Ballin
Teaches not just the mechanics, but the art of actually "speaking" through improvisation to tell the listener a story. Includes a diskette with a demo of "Band in a Box" software and play-along files of all the exercises in the book. Endorsed by Michael & Randy Brecker, (A computer is not needed to use this book.)
00030027 Book/Diskette Pack $19.95

Technical Exercises for the Intermediate to Professional Jazz Musician
by Jordon Ruwe
Designed to develop technical ability moving through all keys. Embodies the essence of bop for strengthening melodic lines for personal and developmental growth. Chord symbols above each exercise aid in analysis. Clear and concise organization through all 12 keys.
00841047 ....$19.95

Basic Workout Drills for Creative Jazz Improv

by Denis DiBlasio
Covers all the basic musical tools to aid in mastering improvisation. Denis DiBlasio presents helpful ideas he has learned from great players and teachers. This book will move students far forward in their efforts toward mastering the art of practicing. Includes a play-along cassette.
00030037 Book/Cassette Pack.....................$14.95

FOR MORE INFORMATION, SEE YOUR LOCAL MUSIC DEALER,
OR WRITE TO:

HAL•LEONARD®
CORPORATION

7777 W. BLUEMOUND RD. P.O. BOX 13819 MILWAUKEE, WI 53213